Raise from Dust

Poems of our world today
and hope for tomorrow

Alison Stedman

Onwards and Upwards Publishers

3 Radfords Turf,
Cranbrook,
Exeter,
EX5 7DX,
United Kingdom.

www.onwardsandupwards.org

This first edition published in the United Kingdom by Onwards and Upwards Publishers (2016).

ISBN: 978-1-911086-82-6
Typeface: Sabon LT
Graphic design: LM Graphic Design

Printed in the United Kingdom.

About the Author

Alison grew up in Kent, having been born in Devon in the early 60s. She found faith in Jesus at age eleven and her Christian walk has spanned the years, shaping her choices in life and her writing. She trained as a nurse in London at Guy's Hospital and a year after qualifying, went to work at St Christopher's Hospice. In 1987 she felt God was calling her to "go", specifically to the Himalayan kingdom of Bhutan. A door opened through The Leprosy Mission and so she lived there from the end of 1988 to May 1996. Back in the UK she returned to St Christopher's where she worked until her marriage to Bill Leishman, in 2000, took her to Oldham, Lancashire. After the birth of their first son, Samuel, in 2002, Alison became a full time mum. Tom was born two years later. They moved to Douglas, Isle of Man in 2012.

She started writing poems in her early twenties and had *Faith Hope Love* published in 1987, and *The Song of the Sparrow* published in 1991 with a foreword by Princess Diana. She is delighted now after many years of being a busy mum to have another collection published. She hopes that through her writing readers will be comforted and challenged, but above all will be pointed to God who has been with her through the valleys as well as on the mountain tops.

Visit Alison's website at **alisonstedmanpoetry.com**, or simply scan this barcode with your smartphone:

Endorsements

Being a health professional gives a writer a very particular insight into the human condition, an intimate understanding that is necessarily detached, if also sensitive and sympathetic. Being a mother, too, and a Christian, brings further layers of experience and appreciation that loads Alison Stedman's writing with a power to both shock and disarm the reader. We are (sometimes darkly) amused by it, too, and intrigued, inspired, uplifted by the work this wryly observant poet has produced – her collection gives us all life: from the fine focus on a melting snowflake to the broad brushstrokes of history, and a new take on Scripture. Stedman is no stranger to pain, whether it be that of childbirth, or the loss of a loved one, or the imagined suffering of Christ on the cross; equally, however, there is deep joy and faith, in relationships, events and in the natural world. In sparse and economical lines, packed with appeal to the senses and the imagination, Stedman evokes places and people, tells stories, and gives voice to a whole gallery of characters. This is a satisfying book from a poet whose next work will be welcomed.

Geoff Daniel
Poetry Advisor, Association of Christian Writers

In this collection of beautifully crafted poems, Alison captures life in all its stark reality: emotion drips from her expressive words as she, sometimes subtly, paints pictures, revealing the scene before her. These pictures though, come to life and draw the reader in, enabling them to live that reality also. Two of her works particularly stand out for me, 'Dead Ironic' and 'Journey Home'; these I found very moving in their composition, eliciting the feeling of loss as a loved one passes. However, in the second part of her book, 'Raised', we are introduced to a very positive theme; we begin to glimpse hope emerge out of the darkness of despair. Alison encapsulates a beautiful, tender moment in 'Thin Blue Line', as she relates a mother's experience of pregnancy, birth and family life – real life experiences. Then the question, 'What of the future for my children?' We feel the anguish and yet the hope. Finally, Alison revisits, in graphic verse, the events of the Bible's New Testament. Her works culminate in the realisation that God's Kingdom has come on earth through the life, death and resurrection of Jesus Christ – hope comes to a desperately needy world.

Raised from Dust is a book to return to many times. I thoroughly recommend it.

David J. Bailey
Retired Baptist Minister and Author

Thought-provoking yet very accessible, these are poems that will resonate over and over again with the reader. I've found myself coming back to them hours later – pondering on deeper meanings, reflecting on what they have to say about modern life and the people I meet every day, or challenging me about my attitudes and preconceptions. I loved the poems that so vividly portray the Isle of Man, but I also enjoyed those that transported me to bustling cities or exotic faraway places. I read with pleasant nostalgia poems celebrating the precious gift of children and family life and I was deeply touched by those that embrace illness and death. Yet most importantly perhaps, here too are poems that challenge my faith and encourage my often-faltering walk with God; that retell in a new way stories that are so familiar to me; that reveal once again God's kingdom, and remind me of the depth and power of God's love for the whole world. Thank you, Alison, for such refreshing and inspirational writing.

Jacqueline Shirtliff
Teacher and former editor of Magnet magazine

Contents

To my wonderful husband Bill.

Thank you for all your faithful love,
support and encouragement over the years.
Your selfless dedication to the Gospel is an inspiration;
I am honoured to be your wife.

&

To Samuel and Tom.

God has truly blessed me by giving me two amazing sons.
I pray that as you continue on life's journey God will bless you
and have His hand on all the plans He has for you.
Thank you for all the love, fun and laughter that you bring.

Foreword by Wendy Craig

*A*lison Stedman has spent her life healing people. She has nursed and comforted the sick and displaced, and given them her help and sympathy.

For many years she worked for The Leprosy Mission in Bhutan as a matron and during a break in England she suffered depression. She recovered, and bravely went back to Bhutan to continue her care of those suffering from leprosy. A year later Alison returned to London and always feeling God's calling on her to help others, she worked at St. Christopher's Hospice, until she met Bill Leishman, a Baptist Minister whom she married a year later. They now live on the Isle of Man and have two teenage sons.

These poems reflect moments and events in her life and express her Christian calling and faithful obedience to the ministry of Christ. They are a deeply moving testimony to her faith and convey great tenderness for the suffering of others as well as awareness of her own strengths and weaknesses and moments of joy and pain.

I found myself uplifted and inspired by her sympathy for humanity and her love for all creation; indeed, she opens the eyes and stirs the heart with her uncomplicated and free-flowing verse. I'm so grateful to her for allowing me to read her latest work. It has rekindled in me a desire to stay close to God, and has refreshed my mind with her passionate sentiments and delicate and accurate use of words.

This book is a treasure of human experience and awareness. I intend to always keep it near me to remind me of God's provision and the beauty and diversity of life. Through her poems Alison continues her healing ministry, and it is beyond price.

Wendy Craig
Star of British TV

Dust

Change?

"Change, please?
Any change, please?"
Sitting hunched,
Blanket huddled,
Eyes dull, downcast.
Stained cap,
Upturned in hope
On cracked paving slab.
Monotone voice, repeating
Endlessly the same,
Day after day,
Lived-in shoes
Pass him by,
Leaving him behind,
No change...
No change.

Checkout Call

The ringing broke in,
the shopping queue shuffled to a halt.
We simultaneously reached for our mobiles,
but it was hers this time.
Her face crumpled with
news she'd dreaded,
the cashier continued scanning and loading
everyday groceries into carriers.
Apologetic, the cashier looked up for the payment.
"It's my sister," the tear-stained woman said,
"they are working on her."
Not a place to get news like this
in the glare of the day-to-day
when the conveyor belt of life endlessly trundles along.
"I had good news yesterday,"
blurted out the cashier,
"no further treatment needed."
When my turn came,
I had no intimacies I wanted to share.
I stacked shopping carefully into bags
while sending up silent prayers for the shaken woman
    and her sister,
and thanking God that He can even use us to pray
in supermarket queues.

The Swarm

Listen,
in the distance,
reverberating through spring island air,
is a hum.
A repetitive drone,
as if millions of bees
on tiny silvery wings
are invading
the tranquil evening
of Ellan Vannin.

The monotonous noise
demanding attention
is no natural inhabitant,
but an annual phenomenon.
Tourist Trophy racers and
global visitors
are released in their droves,
swarming the island.
Like an injection of party hype,
pulsating engines
and fairground noise,
spreads through the veins
transforming island life.
Constant buzz,
rev of engines,
leathered bikers astride
glistening multicoloured machines,
morph into a new deadly creature of
man, machine and speed.

As the world focuses in
on the padded route
at the island's heart;
watching racers flash past,
helmets on, visors down,
knees gripping seats,
hanging on to defy grim death
...the island becomes hypnotised.

While beds and bars fill up
and cash machines run dry,
honey drips through the fingers
of the locals,
sticky and sweet.
But drivers and pedestrians
beware,
this seasonal harvest
comes with a cost,
five fatalities this year
the sting in the tail.

The Plot

Tonight expectation hangs in the air
with a hint of bonfire and
dank autumn leaves.
As sun sets
toffee apple colours
stick to mackerel clouds,
a prelude to stars cascading across the night.
Bright-eyed children wait,
gloved and padded,
little voices shrill,
enduring parents' last preparations.

In hooded coats,
they trip out,
old gloves grip magic wand sparklers.
With delighted squeals lights are painted into crisp air.
A picture that stays longer in memories
than the stick whose orange glow fizzles to grey,
dropped spent, abandoned on the path.

For one night,
neighbourhoods fill with flashes and crackles,
dripping colour down from sky bursts,
to offer a half-remembered reminder
of long ago history.
Rebellion and a murder plot,
terrorism and treason failed.
A king spared,
a gang of men tortured
then swung from a gallows,

on a night as cold as this,
with an expectant crowd,
looking on for grim entertainment.
Surely no place for children.

Pebble Protests

Small world frustrations
drop like pebbles,
rings ripple out
through a once calm morning
from a tender heart.

Tears well up
in his eyes,
to underline the strength of feeling.
Child to parent protest
that has been weighed
by adult wisdom
and fallen short of reason.

Strong will pounds
like clenched fists in a fight,
against the protective barriers
invisible to children
but there to keep them safe
in a lawless world,
where anything goes if you let it.

"You don't understand,"
pins the blame always
on the mystery of parenthood.
Maybe I did once,
as the child in me reflects
on my pebble protests
now long ago forgotten
drops in the ocean.

Red Alert

She came,
heavy with shopping,
red scarf waving secret messages
on seaside gusts.
She stood poised,
car park deserted,
lowered bags to her feet.

Before she declared her generous intention,
they seemed to know.
Appearing one by one, at first,
noiselessly landing on walls, fences.
Careful,
surrounding at a safe distance,
the reconnaissance.
Beady eyes watching, wings folded,
side-stepping with edgy deliberation,
beaks pointed towards her,
hopeful.

She reached down,
tugged open plastic wrapping.
In that instant the sky was full,
a flurry of white and grey wings,
the fleet circling, hovering, swooping.
As she cast her donation around
with jerks of urgency,
yellowed beaks snatched and squawked ravenous menace,
in a stabbing fury.

Trying to share fairly
to this vast clamouring crowd,
she cast handfuls to the young and bespeckled
and cunning old alike.
They trespassed too close, alighting on her back,
but she continued her quest,
until every last crumb,
flung and fought over.

With greedy ingratitude,
they left her alone,
lifting off indifferently into salt-sea air,
a retreating cloud, smug,
mission accomplished.
Calling only to each other,
gone, gone.

Tucking the flapping scarf
safely into her coat,
carriers gathered up,
she ambled away,
job done.
That frenzied scene
over in a moment.
But up high, unnoticed,
the scavenging sentries perch,
on cliffs or chimney pots,
guarding 'their' town;
ever watching, waiting,
for the next signal.

Extra Pegs

Weather warning,
pendulous swing of the hanging basket.
Innocent mackerel sky
yet beneath, sways and gusts
gather leaves and toss them with uncaring abandon.
Open windows tap a wild rhythm
as nets are sucked and billowed back.
Fuchsia stems bob,
sending pink dancing ladies twirling and jiving.
The hint of sunshine draws damp washing
to be hung flapping like a tethered creature,
that needs to be tamed with extra pegs.
It strains on its leash,
tugging, waiting to wrench away,
to make a bid for freedom over the fence.
Flapping wet wings
twist and pull,
until pegs drop defeated
and it dives sodden,
triumphant into a corner,
back to the dirt.

Storm

Fighting to stand.
Hood and coat hugged tightly,
against buffeting wind.
Drawn like a magnet to be there,
to experience the force of the elements.
Immense power transforming picturesque island tip
into a wild, dangerous scene.
Looking over the edge
at surging water, relentlessly pounding the cliff,
foaming up the gullies.

Seagulls grounded
stand around bemused between the puddles
caught between wiry tussocks.

A young couple
run past me, hand in hand
recklessly towards the edge.
I smile at their
joie de vivre.

The swirling air is heavy,
saturated with salt
whipped up from the waves,
like wild bath foam.
In desperation of somewhere to rest
it clings to lips and skin.

I try to hold the moment in a photo,
but it freezes the experience,
silences the roar,
pinning it down like a captured dead butterfly.

As I battled with each step
from the safety of the building,
I knew that here was a glimpse of Creator God's power,
who spoke and made sea and sky
come into being with His powerful word,
and who in a whisper can calm the wind and waves,
or hold me safe through life's storms
    in the palm of His hand.

Mountain Snowfall

Snow clouds hanging low
smothering the valley
putting a lid on the world.
A still hush falls
with every flake
burying sounds in muffled softness.
The mountain rests with its people
as the winter hug enfolds the slopes
in a white sleep.

Only as the fingers of light
poke through,
is untouched silence broken.
Stroke of warmth
reversing each flake
to fluid;
sound to movement.
A monotonous
drip, drip, drip
builds up momentum,
as the roof lets go its grip
and snow slides into slush
seeping away deep into the earth.
Then all that's left
is the rush of the river
slicing into the valley below.

Manannan's Cloak

Somewhere a single muffled hoot sounds
as the steam train slowly slides out of town
like a ghost.
Today a thick curtain hangs
a wall like wet cotton wool,
grey and close,
dank and clammy,
hugging the streets and back lanes.
The damp silence
is broken briefly,
by a fog horn and
the plaintive cry of a gull
sulking up on a chimney pot unseen above.

Maybe today Manannan has risen up again
out of the sea,
wrapping his protective cloak
and holding possessively in its folds
his love
Ellan Vannin.
Today she is his
and his alone,
engulfed and hidden
from the outside world,
he jealously guards her shores.

But,
a dagger of sunlight
tears through,
splitting the clouds.

He tries to hold on
but his grip is lost with every warm ray of sun,
he is pushed back into the deep.
Leaving tattered, torn remnants of cloak,
hanging in the valleys.
As the threads dissolve under the sun's
triumphant gaze,
Ellan is free again.

Emerald Buddha

Gold glistens in fish scales
over the columns.
Painted roof with winged edges
like the curled, expressive dancer's hands
pointing skyward.
Sandalwood sticks burn,
distinctive aroma spirals up
to blend with humid city air.
In amongst all this Eastern elegance
and ancient worship,
the tourists shuffle,
with cameras and straw hats.
They pose next to grimacing stone demons
with green-toothed masked faces.
And inside its golden shrine
the emerald Buddha looks down
at millions of pilgrims and visitors,
with closed eyes
and a stone heart;
he doesn't see, he's blind,
but still the people bow, gaze and pay.
Then at the end of the day
his saffron-robed servants
scoop up the money
making space for the next day's homage.

Karigiri Sunset

The last tinge of soft gold
spills along the horizon.
A cascade of birds
whirl
swirl
circling
dropping
to their roost.

The last of the warm wind
whispers
breathes
through raffia palm leaves.
It hums to earth,
rock and mountain,
soothing and gentle as a sigh.

The last triumph of colour
paints bushes flame red
and burns the ground terracotta,
before day slips away.
Dripping darkness,
cool,
inky black.

Dark Shadows

So tired
too tired
everything in slow motion
the world is a blur,
out of focus.
A widening gulf
between me and you.
But please be there for me
nothing to say or do
– just be,
and let me just be, too;
no demands
no expectations.

Feeling numb inside
face and voice expressionless.
When the fuse blew
balanced emotion was washed away
in a salty torrent.
Now each word
… delayed reaction.
People out there talk
… try to catch
… each word,
concentrate
– no, missed it again.
Better not to listen
better to be alone,
but frightened to be left alone…
in case…

I must hide away
hibernate...
hibernate and sleep.
Fight to sleep
and fight to wake up
in the morning.
Another day to get through.
Why get up?
Try to get up,
drag myself up,
but the heavy blurriness
is still there.
Will it be gone tomorrow?
Do the dark shadows ever disappear?

Dead Ironic

We sat on the bed
looking at the Telegraph crossword.
The clue was:
"punctual?
late?
or very punctual?"

We paused for thought.
I got the answer
then wished I hadn't,
"Dead on time."
"Yes," he said.
We sat in silence
as I inked it in.

It could have been
a conversation opener, but...
we both knew it was ironic...
Time for him was nearly up.
The daily crossword
was there to pass the time...
...what little he had left,
before he would be
very punctual
but known as late.

Journey Home

Gratefully I spot
one space left,
squeezed between a youth,
thumbs punching texts,
overalls spattered magnolia and
a hunched, wrinkled woman
fiercely clutching her handbag
as if her whole world was inside.
A stream of children tumble on
filling the aisle,
laughing, pushing, teasing,
weighed down with backpacks,
learning over for the day.
They grip the seat backs
as the bus jerks,
and pulls away.

As I gaze through murky windows
at London streets,
I see only the people who filled my day.
In the corridor
a man unexpectedly
crumpled,
bled and died.
Shaken,
we scooped him up,
wheeled him
to the privacy of a side room,
washed off sticky clots,
changed his clothes,

made him neat, presentable,
ready for a shocked family;
who didn't think it would be that quick.

I sat with an elderly mother,
who tried to brush away weary tears
as she gripped her dying son's hand.
Her questions unanswered
as to why it was him first
and not her.

A husband,
numb and silent,
watched his wife slip into unconsciousness,
while wishing he could put into safe words,
all that he felt he wanted to say to her
before...
but too afraid of unlocking
the uncontrolled torrent of feelings
that could drown him.

Now I was out
in the bustle of an unknowing world,
where we all go about our daily lives
as if time here is endless,
and life is ours to waste.
Here on the bus,
no-one would guess
that today I was privileged to travel
with some,
as they reached their final stop,
and stood alongside
those who were there
to wave goodbye.

Raised

Little Miracle Girl

Held in his arms
the little big-eyed girl,
so still, so silent.
Down the twisting track,
to the hospital,
carried in desperation,
seeking a Western cure.

A father lined with concern,
laid her gently before us.
She had been shaken,
her mind jolted by seizures
that had gripped her
too many times.
Now frozen, body limp,
she lay gazing up at us,
dazed, confused.

While we waited and watched,
he heard about a different sort of God;
a God who cares,
a God who touches lives,
a God who can heal.
At his request
we gathered around them,
asked our Heavenly Father
to awaken her sleeping mind.

There was no sudden flash,
no leap, no lightning,
no pick-up-your-bed-and-walk moment.

Instead the miracle unfolded
gentle as spring,
pushing through winter earth.
The next day,
beautiful as an opening bud,
she sat up,
lifted shaky hands to eat her rice.
Another day, she stood.
He walked her round the bed,
his arms under hers.
Their eyes reflected
the smiles of hope
as she gradually came back to life.

When he took her hand
led her back up the track
home again, restored;
we knew we had seen
a rare wonder,
an encouragement to our faith,
and the first steps
at the beginning of his,
because he now believed too.

Status Update

Cold rain lashed across the road,
wind fought to snatch the umbrella.
Soaked jeans clung
and yet a warm glow filled me.
I strode on, joy bubbling inside,
because I had seen the answer.

In February
the message had pinged onto my screen,
from an on-line friend
known long ago during her childhood
when we both lived as neighbours in a faraway place.
A request to pray, a longing,
to end a five-year wait.

Internet now linked us across continents,
lives reconnected,
"Please pray, we don't yet have a baby,"
she whispered by technology.
A sister's plea fuelled by faith
and the knowledge that our Heavenly Father
can do the impossible.

Putting off braving the downpour
I dipped into social media,
peeped into other lives
interlocked through invisible lines.
And suddenly there she was
sleeping peacefully in a status update,
twenty days old,
warm and snug somewhere in India.

Here was a cold December morning
but it was a wonderful warm spring of praise
that welled up inside me.
My friend's wait was over,
the answer was a "yes"
whom I could see asleep and amazing.

Over the years ahead
I hope my screen will bring
snapshots of this new life as she grows,
longed for and loved.
Each time I will give a prayer of thanks,
and I'll remember the day
when I laughed against the rain.

Thin Blue Line

We knelt together
wet white stick
dripping amber,
maybe...
Then the message came;
pause of wonder,
tears of joy.
The message said,
"I am here,"
hidden inside my secret place,
that nourishing growing space,
tiny, just beginning.
Heart, mind and life expanding;
"I am here, notice me."

That was the first time
we knew you to be,
wondered who you'd become,
began to wait,
began to love.

Steadily you swelled me,
took from my nourishment,
pushing out the walls of your space
as you strengthened and grew.
I whispered to you
and you answered,
at first a fluttering
like a hovering butterfly.

Later a pummelling of fists and feet,
a heel or elbow
rippling the surface,
strong and bold.
I could almost see you,
almost hold your hand.

We marvelled at
your pounding heart,
echoing, clear and loud,
around hospital walls.
Then squinted at you,
curled up, mouth pouting,
in black and white,
as you tried to wriggle from the sound waves.
That blurred image proudly pocketed
knowing you are beautiful.

You rested,
waited two extra days than expected
in your watery cocoon.
Until it burst and began to leak out.
Then the pain full of purpose gripped me,
carrying me along on a tidal wave
that would finally break,
as you came crashing out,
propelled into cold air,
full of colour and life.
You cried and gasped
as your lungs shouted their independence,
in your bid for freedom.

I took you
flaying arms, puffy face,
mottled and covered in mess and confusion,
and held you in my arms
skin to skin at last.
I savoured the details
of your scrunched face and little fists,
as I cradled you,
my golden-haired boy.
The umbilicus clamped and severed
stopped pulsing,
its job done.
That lifeline now redundant
as you learn your first lesson of life,
to suckle for your own nourishment.
The ties of love can never be cut between us,
even when, one day,
your independence is complete.

Over the years we are still watching,
seeing you gradually emerge
into the young man,
whose body was formed in that quiet space.
Still praying and waiting
to see God unfold the plan
He mapped out for you.

The thin blue line
a powerful message,
a pregnant pause,
the start of life's road
that only God sees beyond the horizon.

Privilege

As the dust settles,
traffic jams dispersed,
derailed trains and building blocks
swept away into boxes;
adult space is reclaimed.
Calm slips in gradually with evening
as jostling activity fuelled by active minds
is soothed into rest by lavender bubbles.
Favourite pyjamas, hugs and stories,
minty toothpaste smiles, gaps admired,
pen marks scrubbed and bruises caressed.
Prayers and worries of the day, shared,
placed into Jesus' hands.
Downstairs, a sigh, a coffee
pause in motherly activity.
Then tiptoeing back
to steal a gaze,
watching each in turn.
Heads with hair tousled on pillows,
limbs abandoned.
A mother's privilege,
secret moment to drink in the peace.
Soft light shows smiles and frowns
dissolved by sleep,
tears and scuffles all resolved.
Long lashes rest on velvet soft cheeks,
years roll back as
baby pouts return and
gentle rhythm of breathing
whispers all is well.

Asleep and beautiful are my sons
with the murmurings of dreams on their lips,
as still deep within imaginations stir,
crafting games,
processing the adventure which is life,
where good-guy superheroes always win
and the world is saved again.

Brainstorming

Our walk together is filled
with the constant stream of imagining.
Cogs turning as inventions
are described in amazing detail,
crafted in your mind.
Explained with hands and intense expressions.
Traffic passes unseen and other pedestrians
curve their paths around us in their ordinary lives.
School-bag swings with each gesticulation,
I listen and smile.

I am privileged to be your confidant,
of bold thoughts and future projects;
love and pride sweep over me again.
One day the power of your inquisitive mind,
your passion for facts and numbers
which today tumbles out in childlike chaos,
will be channelled and used in a world that needs you.
But, my little inventor,
you will grow up
to find that the mundane, bread-and-butter of life,
    takes priority.
But don't lose that spark, my son,
of drive to change the world.
Make it a better place with what's in your head
    and your heart.

"I want to be a primary school teacher, a mathematician
or an inventor."
Some day you may be one of these
or do something as yet unknown.

Wherever your mind's meandering takes you,
however life works out for you,
I will always treasure our walks together
and remember listening to your ideas flowing
and will smile a mother's smile.

The Light of Life

Here candles are lit again.
Gentle glow, flickering light,
familiar occasion.
A pause to honour
the Christ child.
A timeless God
who plummeted to our world
to grow in a womb
to live, hurt and die
and in rising to break the mould of death,
become unsnuffable everlasting light,
a light to outshine all lights,
a light to banish darkness,
a light to pass on.

Our time here slips by
year by year
like melting wax.
This year almost ended
and here we are again:
old familiar tunes,
songs about shepherds and kings,
remembering the child newborn
in a manger.

When you leave here
step out into dark, damp, cold air,
candles snuffed out for another year,
will you leave the light behind?
or will you carry Him with you
in your inmost self?

Like hands cupped round the precious flame
against the winds of fear and doubt.
Will you let Him lead you,
guide you,
take you into the unknown
of the year to come?

Then
when rivulets of hot wax
have turned hard and cold,
when your life's wick
has burned to a stub,
will you be carrying
the Christ-light
within you
into eternity?

On Eagles' Wings

Tired, battle-weary, ragged,
I came to you, Lord,
and waited;
rested in you.
Snow-capped mountains loom,
unreachable above the rocky ledge.
Here I paused,
drank in your peace,
to let your strength
begin to fill and refresh me.

Then the wind began to blow
channelled along the valley.
You sent your Holy Spirit
warm and powerful.
I spread my wings again
gentle breeze ruffling feathers in anticipation.
Leaning towards the invisible strength,
I stepped out
into air updraft, and flew...
riding the current
circling the valley
up... up over the mountains
revealing range after range.
Piercing sky above,
vast endless vista unfolding
in the fullness of your world.

Isaiah 40:29-31

Highly Favoured

Wood smoke curled into night air,
oil lamps in windows flickered
as day ended.
Dusty, weary travellers
jostled for a resting place,
under a cold, clear sky.
A young girl gripped
her swollen belly,
before moving along in the crowd.
"It's starting," she whispered,
to the man on whose arm she leaned.

On and on they searched,
rejected at every door.
The pain inside intensified,
doubling her up,
catching her breath.
She longed to stop,
yearned to be home with her mother.

Finally,
among the stench of animals,
she started to cry out
as she paced the stable floor.
A frightened teenager crouched and
struggled to push her baby out
into the cold, dirty world.
His high-pitched cry
Came as relief and joy.

Exhausted,
she wiped blood off
crinkled, creased skin,
wrapped the cloth around him,
put him to her breast.
"Jesus," she whispered,
stroking dark hair;
brown eyes looked back
searching her face.

As she held the promise of eternity
close in her arms,
the course of time on earth was changed forever.
And in the heavens above
the light of a burning star
pierced through the darkness.

Loaves and Fishes

To many in the crowd
it would have looked ridiculous,
that the young boy thought his small picnic
could be of any use.
But he stepped forward,
offered what he had.
He could have shared it with a few,
or eaten it all himself,
but because he gave it all to you,
it was used, beyond his imagination.

Lord,
teach me to offer to you,
without reservation,
or hesitation, in faith,
the loaves and fishes of my life:
my thoughts,
my words,
my actions,
my hopes,
my future.
Take them,
give thanks and bless them.
Break them and share them.
So my little lunch-box life,
in your hands
can become part
of your overflowing feast.

Out of the Boat

We are in limbo,
undulating water of uncertainty
moves under our feet.
Waves and wind more real here
than when the safety of a wooden hull
hugged our cowering souls.

We heard you call,
took that first unbelievable step,
trusting it was your voice.
This step
the hardest,
depending on your guidance in our hearts, while
flaying arms wave a protest of reason in our minds.

Above deep water
we walk forward
trying to keep you in our vision.
Looking to your reassuring beckoning,
yet buffeted by doubts
that threaten to sink us.

We are out of the boat
so lead us on
even though our steps are hesitant
and our destination uncertain,
let our direction always be
towards you.

After the Rain

Dankness hangs in the air.
The earthy scent rich, dark
rises like a sigh,
after the rain.

Sodden leaves speckle grass.
Trees cling with giant alien hands to slopes,
sucking life, clinging on.
Pearly drips totter,
waiting,
poised to drop on unsuspecting passers-by.
Velvety moss coats tree trunks
like a shabby worn glove.

Worms too near the surface
are soon tugged, rubber-banded
into eager beaks.

The sky, a moving patchwork of clouds,
rushes on;
blue hope jostling,
with grey being finally ousted,
freeing a sunburst
to crown the park
in shimmering splendour.

When Trading Ceased

Feathers flew
as wings escaped cages.
Sheep and young heifers jostled to flee
from tumbling tables,
when the whip-crack split the air.
Burst bags,
spewed coins clattered down,
onto a manured yard.

Chaos,
farmyard sounds and
enraged dealers' protests
filled the air,
as trading ceased for the day.

The righteous anger
of God's son, Jesus,
had come.
He took charge
as high priest,
as promised Messiah;
cleansing his father's house,
redeeming the space for all nations.

This living temple said,
no more exploitation,
no more exclusion.
My father's house shall be
a place of prayer for all.

John 2:12-23

For God So Loved the World

Wood splintered
agony shrieked
blood released
pulsing out,
hammering of metal
bones jerked
sinews, muscles
twisted and stretched.

Long hours...
minute... by... minute
second... by... second
breath... by... breath,
every heave of the ribcage
a struggle.

Heat
thirst,
"I am thirsty."
Bitter vinegar!

Crowds shouting
soldiers quarrelling.

Drifting in... and out... of consciousness.
Voices below... hazy.
Women weeping.

A distant city,
A hurting world,
A fallen humanity.
"Father, forgive them."

Darkness,
So much darkness.
Heaviness inside
all around.
Staring into the abyss
a never-ending tunnel of despair.
Evil, echoing
filling thoughts with nightmare images:
wars, disease, holocaust
anger, bitterness, pride,
lust, gluttony,
selfishness,
indifference.
"Where are you, God?
Have you left me?"
Suffering concentrated on Him,
Jesus.

Lungs heave last
sighing breath out.
"It is finished,
receive my spirit."

Colour and life
drain away,
threa-dy heart-beat stops.
Head bows
stillness
corpse.

For God so loved the world
that He gave His only son.

The Women's Journey

Cold,
dark,
morning hours.
Eyes tired, puffy,
stinging from tears,
hearts heavy with grief,
numbed.
Their Lord, dead.
Now slowly,
to the burial site,
they walked.
To anoint Him,
wrap Him,
weep at His feet again,
for the last time.
Silence of shared memories,
enveloped them.
The long hours of agony,
haunted them,
as their journey began.

Warmth,
light,
flickered, as sun's rays
filtered over the tombs.
Pale whispers of hope,
danced off cold stones of death,
as a new day dawned.
They saw the tomb,
empty of death.

Lightening angels proclaiming,
"He has risen,"
dissolved long shadows of grief,
as realisation flooded
into their hearts,
transforming them into the first messengers
of new life.
Their direction changed.

Red hot
astounding news,
sent them running.
Hearts thundering,
voices tripping over with joy.
A compulsion to share:
"We know He has risen!"
Back to tell the others
and everyone...
onward;
a journey down through history
to us
and the ends of the earth.

Raised from Dust

Lifeless and empty,
from the dust of the earth,
humankind was moulded.
Lovingly mixed particles,
fashioned and designed,
masterpiece masterminded.
Then Creator God's life-breath,
Holy wind,
filled them,
transforming them into being.
Body, soul, mind, complete,
united and perfect.
Woven with unique gifts;
an eternal soul,
a seeking mind,
and the freedom of choice.
Man of dust was given life,
love and purpose.
Commissioned to cherish creation
he walked hand in hand,
heart to heart with Creator God;
truly worshipping Him and
harmonising with all creation.
God's kingdom was earth.

But when the decayor
offered the tiny seed of rebellion,
man of dust chose to let it grow;
rooting deep into his very being.

Pride, selfishness and greed germinated,
infecting the perfect design
of body, soul and mind.
Strangling,
pushing out the Holy wind,
until pure life-breath was squeezed away and
the perfect Creator bond snapped!
The whole of creation
came toppling down
into the mire of death,
and began to rot.
Destruction and pain's epidemic
spreading throughout creation and history,
and righteous Creator God's heart was pierced.

However,
Creator's pure love
couldn't be tarnished,
because it is His very being;
So great was it for man of dust still.
He knew there was only one
selfless solution:
to uproot decayor's curse,
to restore, reconcile, recreate;
to come Himself as dust-created
yet filled with Holy breath wind.
So Jesus was spoken
into the ruined masterpiece.
Into the mire of decayed world He was born.
Yet with no trace of selfish seed.

In humility He led,
with wholeness He healed,
dust-created yet full of the force of Holy wind.
Then in selfless love,
He chose to grasp decayor's root,
pulling it into Himself.
Breaking the strangle hold
decayor's power was broken,
giving back the key of choice
to man of dust.
Imprisoned eternal being
could be unlocked
as Jesus became the new gateway
to God's kingdom.
Flung open as arms
spread wide
impaled on the cross.
The deadly power of decayor's seed
crushed forever
as the power of the Holy breath
rolled away the stone of death.
Jesus rose to lead
dust-humankind into reclaimed kingdom.
Hope reborn in all creation.

So now Creator's promise,
the Holy wind is rebreathed
into all who choose Jesus.

Throughout time,
across the world
the new created man is found;
cell by cell,
a body of many parts
functioning in unity
with Jesus as head.
A people from many nations
filled, recommissioned
Creator pulsing
the kingdom body into life.
Mobilizing into action
each cell, each limb,
to work in harmony.
Sent to step out into a broken world
to speak as His voice,
call to the lost;
heal with His touch
the broken and hurting
and to stand with arms lifted up,
pointing towards Creator God,
Redeemer Son,
Empowering Holy Spirit.

For God's kingdom is come
on earth again.

Ephesians 2
Colossians 1:15-24